Angels, wise men, a baby. Why doesn't God show himself more clearly?

IF GOD IS THERE, why doesn't he make himself more obvious? Apparently he wants people to believe in him, so perhaps this year he could carve a hundred-mile-wide message in the moon: **"Happy Christmas! Love, God."**

More seriously, how can so much be at stake when the evidence appears so underwhelming?

The famous atheist philosopher Bertrand Russell was once asked what he would say if he found himself standing before God on the judgement day, and God asked him, "Why didn't you believe in Me?" Russell replied:

"I would say, 'Not enough evidence, God! Not enough evidence!'"[1]

What do we mean when we say: "There's not enough evidence"? Not enough for what? Not enough evidence to compel someone to become a Christian?

Friedrich Nietzsche made a similar complaint:

"A god who is all-knowing and all-powerful and who does not even make sure his creatures understand his intention – could that be a god of goodness? Who allows countless doubts and dubieties to persist, for thousands of years, as though the salvation of mankind were unaffected by them, and who on the other hand holds out the prospect of frightful consequences if any mistake is made as to the nature of truth? Would he not be a cruel god if he possessed the truth and could

**behold mankind miserably
tormenting itself over the truth?**

**"But perhaps he is a god of
goodness notwithstanding – and
merely *could* not express himself
more clearly!"**[2]

Nietzsche lays down the gauntlet: why
doesn't God impose faith on all
mankind? Maybe you agree with him;
maybe you want coercive proof? But
God does not coerce us into belief. He
has given evidence which is sufficiently
clear for those with an open mind and
heart, but insufficient to compel those
whose hearts and minds are closed.
And if this sounds disingenuous, here
are two significant problems with
overwhelming, coercive proof:

First, does coercive proof really produce
belief that is deep, *authentic* and
lasting?

When I lived in London, I was talking to a
young man I'll call Andy who seemed to
be searching for God. His complaint was
similar to Bertrand Russell's "not enough

evidence". I asked him to imagine what would happen if, that evening, God gave him an overwhelming sign – perhaps by speaking to him in an audible voice but mediated through his cat. Would that really produce genuine faith and trust in God? In a flash, Andy agreed that this would not work and proceeded to tell me about the time he and some gap year friends had an audience with the spoon-bending Uri Geller on a kibbutz in Israel.

"It was weird," Andy said, **"we were all watching in awe as our watches spun backwards and jewellery on our hands and neck became hot and fell off. We knew we had witnessed something remarkable. But back home, a couple of years later when we had a reunion, not one of us still believed in Uri Geller – we had all dismissed the experience as a trick even though no one could explain it."**

The second problem with coercive proof arises when we realise that God is not merely interested in convincing us of his existence (as if he had nothing better to do than to exist) but that he actually loves us and wants a genuine relationship with us.

Naked displays of power are unlikely to win our love and loyalty, as we see played out in the cinema with our super heroes such as Batman or Daredevil. At some stage, these powerful figures are taken for granted by the locals and then despised if they are too heavy-handed on their enemies.

How could God ever win our love if he imposed himself on us with pyrotechnics or weird miracles? How could we ever really love someone so terrifyingly unequal to us, who delights to show off his power?

God in disguise?

Perhaps, like a super hero assuming an alter ego, God could win our love and loyalty by wearing a disguise. Maybe that would work?

With that in mind, imagine that Bill Gates' wife Melinda dies and, some years later, Bill Gates falls in love again, not with a close friend or business associate but one of the cleaners at his Microsoft offices.

How could genuine love flourish? How could Bill Gates be sure the cleaner genuinely loved him rather than his wealth and power?

Bill's plan is simple. He disguises himself as another cleaner in his own Microsoft offices and so, over the weeks and months of cleaning loos and emptying bins, he tries to win her love. Having won her affections and now confident she loves the penniless cleaner he has pretended to be, Bill Gates invites her to his $200m property in Washington State where, with the help of his family and staff, he throws off the disguise and reveals his true identity.

And they both lived happily ever after … or not?[3]

Is that legitimate and honest? Would the cleaner not feel deceived and demeaned? The man she thought she loved only existed in the imagination of Bill Gates, who wears costumes and disguises simply to get what he wants?

"Do I really know him? Can I trust him?" she would ask. "He clearly did not trust me enough to relate to me genuinely, for fear I might be after his money."

The parable of the King and the Maiden

The 19th-century Danish philosopher, Søren Kierkegaard, explored this idea in the Parable of the King and the Maiden:

Suppose there was a king who loved a humble maiden .... For love is overjoyed when it unites equals, but it is triumphant when it makes equal that which was unequal. Let the king's love reign!

But then there arose a sadness in the king's soul. Who would have dreamed of such a thing except a

king with royal thoughts! He spoke to no one about his sadness. Had he done so, each courtier would doubtless have said, "Your Majesty, you are doing the girl a generous favour for which she could never thank you enough." ... Would the maiden really be happy? Would she be able to forget what the king wished to forget, namely, that he was the king and she a former lowly maiden? For if this happened, if the memory of her former state awoke within her, and like a favoured rival, stole her thoughts away from the king – where then would the glory of their love be? She would have been happier had she remained in obscurity, loved by one of her own kind.

But God, the unselfish king, would find no satisfaction in this. He knows ... the maiden, would be gravely deceived. For no deceit is so terrible as when it is unsuspected, when a person is, as it were, bewitched by a change of costume.[4]

The Bible tells us that God is personal, loving and wishes to reach down to humans, whom he deeply loves, and in turn seeks to win our love and trust and unite us to him forever.

Overwhelming us with coercive proof of his power will not win our love, and deceiving us with a disguise will not win our trust.

But to add to all this, God faces a further obstacle: we humans have ransacked his creation, and rejected his authority, forfeiting any right to live forever with him. So how does he reveal himself to us in such a way that we are neither overwhelmed nor deceived? And how then can he forgive us for what we have done and guarantee our future with him?

Blaise Pascal, the famous philosopher and scientist, put it this way:

"Willing to appear openly to those who seek him with all their heart, and to be hidden from those who flee from him with all their heart, God so regulates the knowledge of

himself that he has given indications of himself which are visible to those who seek him and not to those who do not seek him. There is enough light for those to see who only desire to see, and enough obscurity for those who have a contrary disposition."[5]

When **myth** became **fact**

C.S. Lewis, as a committed atheist, dismissed the story of the incarnation as a myth – a beautiful and compelling story, but no different from those of all religions. Helped by his fellow Oxford dons, J.R.R. Tolkien and Hugo Dyson, he gradually realised that not only was this the most beautiful and romantic of all stories but, unlike the others, it was historically true. The incarnation was the myth that became fact:

"If ever a myth had become a fact, had been incarnated, it would be just like this. And nothing else in all literature was just like this. Myths were like it in one way. Histories were like it in another, but nothing was simply alike. And no person was like the Person it depicted; as real, as recognizable, through all that depth of time ... yet also so

luminous, lit by a light from beyond the world, a god. But if a god – we are no longer polytheists – then not a god, but God. Here and here only in all time the myth must have become fact; the Word, flesh; God, Man. This is not 'a religion', nor 'a philosophy'. It is the summing up and actuality of them all."[6]

Each Christmas, all over the world, millions of people consider this story by listening to a reading of John's Gospel, a famous eyewitness account of Jesus' life written by one of his closest followers:

"In the beginning was the Word, and the Word was with God, and the Word was God. He was with God in the beginning. Through him all things were made; without him nothing was made that has been made. In him was life, and that life was the light of all mankind. The light shines in the darkness, and the darkness has not overcome it. [...]

"He was in the world, and though the world was made through him, the world did not recognise him. He came to that which was his own, but his own did not receive him. Yet to all who did receive him, to those who believed in his name, he gave the right to become children of God – children born not of natural descent, nor of human decision or a husband's will, but born of God. The Word became flesh and made his dwelling among us. We have seen his glory, the glory of the one and only Son, who came from the Father, full of grace and truth."[7]

John claims that God, the Word, has made his dwelling with us, neither overwhelming us – **"the world did not recognise him"** – nor deceiving us with a disguise: **"To all who did receive him he gave the right to become children of God ... we have seen his glory, the glory of the one and only Son, who came from the Father, full of grace and truth."**

Jesus never overwhelmed his friends or enemies, but always gave them space to walk away from him. Neither did he hide his glory and identity from those who loved him – only to surprise them with his true identity after his resurrection.

Unlike Bill Gates in the story above, Jesus won the love of those who were unequal to him, not by means of a disguise, that he then threw off like a cloak, but by becoming human forever. And by becoming a human being, he has enabled us to understand him in the deepest possible way: no longer as a theological abstraction, but someone we can understand as we do one another.

In the incarnation, God appeared as he is – humble, loving, beautiful and true. And having won people's love and trust, Jesus will remain human for all eternity so that those who love and trust him will grow deeper in their love for the same person.

Knowing God

There were two views around in John's day about how we can know things, two views that still inform how we think today. They are **Rationalism** and **Mysticism**. It's perhaps best framed as the choice between Richard Dawkins' rationalism and Russell Grant's mysticism: do we choose the New Atheism or New Age?

Rationalism says think your way clear – think your way to true knowledge, whereas **Mysticism** encourages an emptying of the mind.

But is it really possible to get to know God by either approach? For that matter, can we get to know anyone that way? Take my brother, for example: what can you, the reader, tell me about him just by using rational thought? You could deduce that he was male and has a sibling, but beyond those basic facts your rational thought processes would not yield very much, would they? You would not gain personal knowledge of my brother that was meaningful and would help you get to know him.

If rationalism doesn't deliver, what about mysticism? Will mysticism help you to get to know my brother?

You might meditate on the concept of a universal brotherhood, project that onto my brother and conclude, "I like to think of Richard's brother as protective, inclusive and non-judgemental."

And so, you enter into a deep personal relationship with your thoughts about my brother.

Ridiculous as that might sound, really intelligent people do that with God all the time. Maybe you sometimes hear yourself saying: "I like to think of God as loving, non-judgemental, the divine spark in all of us. God lets us find him in our own way and is happy with us however we come to him."

And so, you enter into a deep, mystical relationship with your thoughts about God. Mysticism easily becomes a spiritual game of "let's pretend", and is no more useful in getting to know God than for getting to know my brother.

Rationalism gives you no satisfying information about my brother and mysticism tells you nothing that you can trust. As a matter of fact, I don't even have a brother!

If you are to know someone and be sure of what you know about them (that they exist, for instance), they have to take the initiative and reveal themselves to you. They must disclose information about themselves on Facebook, by phone – or ideally face to face. We only get to know people as they reveal information about themselves.

This is why reading a Gospel – an eyewitness biography of Jesus – is so important.

As you relate to what Jesus said and did in John's Gospel, you find yourself relating to Jesus – getting to know him for yourself. Coming to terms with him as he really is, rather than our preconceptions and prejudices of him.

The Apostle John, as an eyewitness, appeals to what he had seen, heard and touched with regard to Jesus. He was familiar with these two views of rationalism and mysticism. As he wrote his first two lines: **"In the beginning was the Word, and the Word was with God, and the Word was God. He was with God in the beginning"** – he was deliberately engaging with both rationalism and mysticism.

He wrote his Gospel because something had happened that had utterly transformed his life – something his brother James was willing to be executed for and something that he was living for.

Significantly, it is in the Middle East, where East meets West, where rationalism meets mysticism. This is where this incredible thing happened.

This is where the Word (the meaning behind the universe) became properly known and experienced.

God revealed

"In the beginning was the Word and the Word was with God and the Word was God."

If we are to know someone they must disclose information about themselves. John's opening could be rendered: **"The Word (Jesus) was with God – face to face and moving towards God."** This is an enigmatic expression of love and fellowship. Jesus was God and yet was in fellowship with his Father, deepening his relationship all the time, moving towards him.

At the heart of the universe, at the centre of reality, there isn't mere existence, but relationship, personhood, love. There never was a time when the Son and the Father and the Holy Spirit were not in a joyful, creative and loving relationship with each other.

This provides the human race with a basis for the way we are and how we feel. Have we ever really been satisfied by Professor Richard Dawkins' view that love, beauty and altruism can be explained away by merely inventing a scientific-sounding word – "memes"? An unobserved virus that we pass on to make our lives more pleasant?

In 2009, a scientific study concluded that kissing was primarily about men passing on saliva to help create immunity in their prospective mates, before they conceived and alien diseases became more dangerous.

Since men are generally taller than women it makes passing on their saliva in the act of kissing much easier.

Is that *all* a kiss is? A useful mechanism for creating immunity in your prospective mates by exchanging microbes in your saliva?

Well, I guess it all depends on whom you are kissing. If it is whiskery Aunt Maud, who greets you every Christmas with a sloppy kiss, you can't help thinking about saliva and microbes can you?

But this is not an adequate explanation when you are kissing the person you love romantically.

According to the first two verses in John's Gospel, at the heart of reality is love and relationship. This is the foundation for human significance. We were made to be like God, made in his image to relate to him and to others he has made. That is very good news indeed. There is a personal, relational God at the centre of reality and our whole purpose in life is to be in relationship with him – to know him individually for ourselves.

So how can this happen? How can we get to know someone so unequal to us without them overwhelming us or deceiving us? We know we can't just think God up through rational thought or connect with him by mystical meditation.

Well, imagine it this way: What if Shakespeare had wanted to meet Hamlet personally and have a relationship with him? How could he do that, since Hamlet is a created figure and Shakespeare is his creator?

The author of the play has to take the initiative – Hamlet clearly can't – and reveal himself through words. Shakespeare would need to write himself into the play as a speaking person, who develops a relationship with Hamlet and gradually reveals his true identity.

Similarly, God has written himself into the human story at this point in history so people like John could know without any doubt that he is who he claims to be.

As John writes this down he isn't saying: "Hey, here's a philosophical idea I dreamed up in the bath – what do you think?"

No, he's saying, "Look, here's an event that happened. Here is a person I've met and got to know, and knowing him has turned my world upside down. Turned the world upside down. What are you going to do about him?"

As John watched Jesus for three years, and saw his footprints on the beach of Galilee, it gradually dawned on him. This was God, walking on his own planet. John and the other followers of Jesus could never be the same again! They were forever changed, and so was human history.

We mustn't think this was easy for the first followers of Jesus to believe. They were 1st-century Jews, who knew that God was spirit and not a man.

They were neither theologically nor psychologically capable of inventing this idea that God became a man. Suggesting that they did strains credulity: accepting it from Jesus himself often proved hard enough!

What convinced them was Jesus himself, whose miracles and teaching – and most of all his resurrection from the dead – showed them that he was God in human form. Therefore, John came to assert:

"The Word became flesh and made his dwelling among us. We have seen his glory, the glory of the one and only Son, who came from the Father, full of grace and truth."

It should be no surprise, then, that Jesus' birth split time in two, and that even the coins in our pocket are dated from this event. It should be no surprise that more millions of people today and throughout history follow Jesus than follow any other figure alive or dead.

God rejected

"He was in the world, and though the world was made through him, the world did not recognise him. He came to that which was his own, but his own did not receive him."

You would think that Jesus' contemporaries would surely have welcomed him into their lives and hearts. For here at last is Immanuel – God with us – the long-awaited Messiah! In Jesus, they saw perfection, humanity as it was meant to be … and it left them feeling inadequate, shamed and foolish. So they shunned him and ultimately tried to destroy him.

According to John's Gospel, once we see who Jesus really is, we will find ourselves either opposing him or worshipping him: there is no middle ground.

Imagine you play tennis at a local club and have become pretty established and respected on the court. Then one day, Andy Murray moves into the area and joins your club. How would you feel? Initially you would be delighted. But once the novelty of playing a world-class player wore off, you might become cross and frustrated at being shown up so dramatically and so regularly. It's one thing never winning a match, but never winning a set or a game makes you feel foolish and discouraged. Far from admiring Murray's near perfection, you would become irritated and critical and would be relieved if the club banned him.

So, unless you welcomed him as your teacher and mentor, you would shun him and oppose him as you would an enemy.

This passage tells us that we naturally react like this to our creator when he takes human form and joins us. We try to put out the brilliant light he shines into our lives, for as we see his perfection, we see our own failures and inadequacies. He comes to his own – but they do not receive him.

We shun this brilliance, like moral cockroaches scuttling for cover of darkness. The events of the first Christmas – God becoming a man – are an unflattering reminder of our flawed human nature.

As will be the events of the next Christmas, when many of us are forced to reflect on how hard it is to get on with those we love most.

The students I work with admit that the Christmas holiday is just about long enough to remind them of why they were so keen to leave home and get to university in the first place. We are out of sorts with ourselves, and we are out of sorts with each other, because we are out of sorts with God.

You see, to ignore and reject God forces us to expect more and more from other relationships. And expecting human relationships to compensate for the gaping God-shaped hole in our lives puts a huge strain on them! However much we love our family and friends, they simply cannot fill that void. How could they compensate for God? The one in whom you live and move and have your being? How could they fill that inconsolable longing?

Our hearts will be restless until they find rest in God. And our human relationships will be strained to breaking point if they are meant to bear that weight of expectation.

The incarnation, the coming of God to earth in Jesus, is God taking the initiative to reveal himself and to rescue us.

It is our natural rejection of God that reveals why Jesus had to come. We are estranged from God; we've greatly offended and provoked him by our selfishness, pride and greed, living on his planet without any regard for him.

If he were not angry at our rebellious behaviour then he would not be good or just, and if he were not offended and provoked by our cold indifference towards him then he would not really love us. Yet that same love leads God to one conclusion: we need to be rescued from this predicament. Matthew, another Gospel writer and eyewitness of Jesus, records this moment before Jesus' birth. An angel instructs Joseph:

"You shall call his name Jesus for he shall save his people from their sins."[8]

God received

"Yet to all who did receive him, to those who believed in his name, he gave the right to become children of God – children born not of natural descent, nor of human decision or a husband's will, but born of God."

In the nativity accounts, it is curious that the infant Jesus was given the truly bizarre gifts, Gold, frankincense and myrrh: not found in the normal Mothercare range. Myrrh is the really troubling one – why would anyone give a baby a jar of embalming fluid – let alone a so-called wise man!?

Imagine (but don't do it) how well it would go down if you gave your friend's baby boy an ornate coffin for his first birthday.

The gift of myrrh shows that even Jesus' manger was overshadowed by his cross. Throughout John's Gospel, Jesus speaks of his "hour of glory". He is aware of an appointment in time – his "hour" to which his whole life is pointing. By the time we get to just over halfway through the Gospel, we are into the last week of Jesus' life. And for the first time, Jesus says that his "hour has come":

"'The hour has come for the Son of Man to be glorified. Very truly I tell you, unless a kernel of wheat falls to the ground and dies, it remains only a single seed. ... Now my soul is troubled, and what shall I say? "Father, save me from this hour"? No, it was for this very reason I came to this hour. ... I, when I am lifted up from the earth, will draw all people to myself.' He said this to show the kind of death he was going to die."[9]

The gift on offer is Jesus himself.

Jesus, the one who was willing to die so that you could receive forgiveness. Who was willing to take your sin, all your rebellion, and clothe you instead in his righteousness, so God could look on you and accept you, so you could be welcomed into an eternal relationship with him.

Jesus, who was willing to face death and give you eternal life, says, **"To as many as receive me, I give the right to become sons of God."** Literally God's heirs – God's children.

In the 1st century rich, childless men would adopt sons to whom they could pass their vast wealth. That's the image here. We are to be welcomed into God's family to share all that is his forever.

This is the greatest love story, the greatest rags to riches story ever told. A story that is not too good to be true, but is good because it is true – the myth become fact.

This gift on offer is enormous and undeserved and also, because it is a gift, it cannot be earned by us. It is free. Free not because it's cheap – our forgiveness was purchased at enormous cost – but free because it has already been paid for. Interestingly, this gift is not easy to receive. In the rags to riches stories we always imagine it would be easy to accept unconditional love and unlimited wealth.

To as many as received him he gave the right to become God's children, inheriting not just forgiveness but eternal life – life in all its fullness that begins now.

But to become God's children we have to come as children. Full of curiosity and with a willingness to trust.

In the weeks leading up to Christmas 2007, my 11-year-old nephew spent most of the time in hospital receiving intensive chemotherapy. Two days after Christmas, David had a scan to see if the tumours on his brain had shrunk.

The on-duty oncologist had bad news for David: far from reducing they had grown and multiplied aggressively.

"Does that mean I'm going to die?" David asked.

"I'm so sorry, David," said the doctor, who was a very kind Chinese man whom David had never met before. "I'm afraid you are going to die."

"Oh, don't be sorry, Doctor," said David, "I'm not afraid of dying. I have a friend called Jesus. He has promised to be with me when I die and take me to be with him in heaven."

The doctor replied, "David, I'm so glad that Jesus is your friend because he is also my friend. He will help you and he will help your mum and dad and sister as well."

Both David and the doctor understood this verse:

"Yet to all who did receive him, to those who believed in his name, he gave the right to become children of God – children born not of natural descent, nor of human decision or a husband's will, but born of God."

It has nothing to do with race, class, education or talent or whether you were brought up Christian or atheist. Receiving this gift has nothing to do with your background or intelligence or class or temperament. It makes no difference whether you are baptised or a churchgoer. It has nothing to do with your human descent or privilege. To as many as received him, Jesus gave the right to be children, adopted heirs into all that is his.

In the incarnation, God has given us enough evidence for us to be confident that he is there and that he loves us. In Jesus, we do not find ourselves overwhelmed by power or deceived by a humble charade. Rather we find ourselves able to know what God is really like, and become his children so we can know him and love him forever. If you want to receive this gift, you may find this prayer helpful.

Prayer

Dear God,

Thank you for showing us how good you are by sending Jesus to live a perfect life.

I'm sorry that I so often don't do what is good and right and that I've ignored you.

Thank you that you dealt with my sin by sending Jesus to die for me.

Thank you that I can be your child and inherit eternal life with you.

I want to receive the Lord Jesus as my saviour and friend and become a follower of him.

Amen

If you have prayed this prayer, speak to a Christian friend or go to our website www.bethinking.org/booklets and email us using "Contact us".

Interesting articles for further reading

www.bethinking.org is UCCF's website which tries to answer questions that people might want to ask before they're ready to trust Jesus and the Bible – here are a few specific resources:

Can the Bible be trusted?
Article:
www.bethinking.org/is-the-bible-reliable/q-how-could-fallible-men-produce-an-infallible-bible
Video:
www.bethinking.org/is-the-bible-reliable/new-evidence-the-gospels-were-based-on-eyewitness-accounts

Am I really a sinner?
Article:
http://www.bethinking.org/christian-beliefs/are-we-sinners

Did the Christmas story really happen?
Article:
http://www.bethinking.org/jesus/truth-in-the-story-of-christmas

Footnotes

1   Wesley Salmon, 'Religion and Science: A New Look
    at Hume's Dialogues' (*Philosophical Studies 33*,
    1978, page 176).

2   Friedrich Nietzsche, *Daybreak*, trans. R.J. Hollingdale
    (Cambridge: Cambridge University Press, 1982,
    pages 89-90).

3   Bill Gates story inspired by a lecture given by Stefan
    Gustavsson at FEUER conference in Prague,
    November 2014.

4   Søren Kierkegaard, *Provocations, Spiritual writings of
    Kierkegaard*, ed. Charles E Moore (Plough
    Publishing, 2002).

5   Blaise Pascal, *Pensées*, section 7, translated and
    introduced by A.J. Krailsheimer (Penguin Classics
    paperback, 1995).

6   C.S. Lewis, *Surprised By Joy* (New York: Harcourt
    Brace Jovanovich, 1955, page 88).

7   John 1:1-5,10-14.

8   Matthew 1:21.

9   John 12:23-24,27,32-33.